D0520817

INDIAN
COOKING

Photography by Peter Barry
Recipes by Mridula Baljekar
Designed by Richard Hawke
Edited by Jillian Stewart

3257
© 1993 Coombe Books
This edition published in 1993 by Coombe Books
for Mulberry Editions, an imprint of Parragon Book Service Ltd.,
707 High Road, Finchley, London N12 0BT
All rights reserved.
Printed in Hong Kong.
ISBN 1 85813 130 8

INDIAN
COOKING

MULBERRY EDITIONS

Contents

Introduction

India is a vast country with a great diversity of climates, cultures, peoples and geography. It is this rich tapestry woven by Indian culture which gives its cuisine its unique place in culinary history.

Indian cuisine has been shaped over the centuries by many forces. Religion, now as in the past, has had a profound influence. There are many different religions practised in India and most of them give some instruction as to the food eaten by followers. Devout Hindus, for example, will not eat beef because Indian mythology depicts the cow as a sacred animal, while Muslims will not eat pork and their religion defines exactly the manner in which animals must be killed for food. The different races which at one time and another have invaded the country also brought their influence to bear on the cuisine. The Mughals from Afganistan brought with them exotic spices and dried fruit and nuts, the Persians contributed the 'Dhansak' style, and the Kashmiris contributed numerous wonderful vegetarian dishes.

Cooking Indian meals is not difficult, it simply takes a little practice to get the mixture of flavourings correct. This in itself has been made much easier by the quantifying of recipes. Indian recipes are generally handed down from one generation to the next, weights and measures were never used and quantities were simply estimated. It therefore took a long period of apprenticeship to become a cook in India. Thankfully for the Western world the ancient recipes have been laboriously quantified and written down to make our apprenticeship far smoother.

It may appear on first glance that Indian cuisine uses a vast amount of different spices, this is true to some extent, but they are used in only small amounts so that once a good range of spices has been bought they will be used time and again in different recipes. It is the different mixture of spices in any Indian dish which gives it its specific character, so don't be tempted to leave any out. The actual method of cooking Indian meals is usually simple and there are very few specific utensils that are needed. Good quality cast-iron pans with tight-fitting lids and a frying pan with a non-stick surface are useful, as is an electric blender, and a coffee grinder to do the job of the traditional grinding stone.

With the exception of sweets, Indian meals are not strictly categorised, although many people find it easier to split them into starters and main meals rather than serve everything at once. What many people find more difficult is deciding on the refreshment to serve. If you wish to serve alcohol with the meal, lager is best, but a well-chilled dry white wine or cider is also suitable. If you wish to be really authentic, serve water with the meal as they do in India.

MEAT SAMOSAS

The ever-popular Samosas make a wonderful treat on any occasion. In India,
they are a familiar sight at wedding receptions and cocktail parties.

MAKES 18 Samosas

2 tbsps cooking oil

2 medium-sized onions, finely chopped

225g/8oz lean mince, lamb or beef

3-4 cloves garlic, peeled and crushed

½-inch cube of root ginger, finely grated

½ tsp ground turmeric

2 tsps ground coriander

1½ tsps ground cumin

½-1 tsp chilli powder

½ tsp salt or to taste

125ml/4fl oz warm water

150g/6oz frozen garden peas

2 tbsps desiccated coconut

1 tsp garam masala

1-2 fresh green chillies, finely chopped and
    seeded if a milder flavour is preferred

2 tbsps chopped coriander leaves

1 tbsp lemon juice

1. Heat the oil over medium heat and fry the onions until they are lightly browned.

2. Add the mince, garlic and ginger. Stir and fry until all the liquid evaporates and adjust heat to low.

3. Add the turmeric, coriander, cumin, chilli powder and salt. Stir and fry until mince is lightly browned.

4. Add the water and the peas, bring to the boil, cover and simmer for 25–30 minutes. If there is any liquid left, take the lid off and cook the mince over medium heat until it is completely dry, stirring frequently.

5. Stir in the coconut, garam masala, green chillies and coriander leaves.

6. Remove from heat and add the lemon juice. Cool thoroughly before filling the Samosas.

For the pastry

225g/8oz plain flour

50g/2oz ghee or butter

½ tsp salt

75 ml/2½ fl oz warm water

Oil for deep frying

1. Add the butter and salt to the flour. Rub in well.

2. Mix a soft dough by adding the water. Knead until the dough feels soft and velvety to the touch.

3. Divide the dough into 9 balls. Rotate each ball between your palms in a circular motion, then press it down to make a flat cake.

4. Roll out each flat cake into 4-inch discs and cut into two. Use each semicircle of pastry as one envelope.

5. Moisten the straight edge with a little warm water.

6. Fold the semicircle of pastry in half to form a triangular cone.

7. Join the straight edges by pressing them hard into each other. Make sure that there are no gaps.

8. Fill these cones with the filling, leaving about ¼-inch border on the top of the cone.

9. Now moisten the top edges and press them hard together.

10. Deep fry the samosas over gentle heat until they are golden brown and drain on absorbent paper.

SEEKH KABABS

Wooden skewers about 6-8-inches long are the best type of skewers for these kababs. You can use metal or steel skewers, but allow the skewers to cool before shaping the next batch of kababs onto them.

MAKES 18 Kababs

Juice of half a lemon

2 tbsps chopped fresh mint or 1 tsp dried or bottled mint

3-4 tbsps chopped coriander leaves

25g/1oz raw cashews

1 medium-sized onion, coarsely chopped

2 small cloves of garlic, peeled and coarsely chopped

1-2 fresh green chillies, finely chopped or minced; remove the seeds if you like it mild

700g/1½lb lean mince, beef or lamb

2 tsps ground coriander

2 tsps ground cumin

1 tsp ground ajwain (ajowan or carum) or ground caraway seeds

½ tsp garam masala

½ tsp Tandoori colour or a few drops of red food colouring mixed with 1 tbsp tomato purée

½ tsp freshly ground black pepper

1 egg yolk

¼ tsp chilli powder

1 tsp salt or to taste

4 tbsps cooking oil

Grind the following ingredients in a coffee grinder

2 tbsps white poppy seeds

2 tbsps sesame seeds

1. Put the lemon juice, mint, coriander leaves, cashews, onion, garlic and green chillies in an electric liquidiser and blend to a smooth paste. Transfer the mixture to a large bowl.

2. Using the liquidiser, grind the mince in 2-3 small batches until it is fairly smooth, rather like a paste. Add the meat to the rest of the liquidised ingredients in the bowl.

3. Add the rest of the ingredients, except the the oil and knead the mixture until all the ingredients are mixed thoroughly and it is smooth. Alternatively, put all the ingredients, except the oil, in an electric food processor and process until the mixture is smooth.

4. Chill the mixture for 30 minutes.

5. Preheat oven to 240°C/475°F, Gas Mark 9. Line a roasting tin with aluminium foil.

6. Divide the kabab mix into about 18 balls, each slightly larger than a golf ball.

7. Mould a ball onto a skewer and form into a sausage shape by gently rolling between your palms (about 4-5-inches long) and place on the prepared roasting tin. Make the rest of the kababs the same way.

8. Brush generously with the oil and place the roasting tin just below the top rung of the oven. Cook for 6-8 minutes. Remove the tin from the oven and brush the kababs liberally with the remaining oil and cook for a further 6-8 minutes.

9. Allow the kababs to cool slightly before removing them from the skewers.

TIME Preparation takes 15-20 minutes, cooking takes 35-40 minutes.

MUTTON PATTIES

MAKES 14 Patties

1kg/2.2lbs potatoes
½-1 tsp chilli powder
1½ tsps salt or to taste
3 tbsps cooking oil
½ tsp fennel seeds
1 large onion, finely chopped
½-inch cube of root ginger, peeled and
    finely grated
2-4 cloves garlic, peeled and chopped or
    crushed
325g/12oz fine lean mince, lamb or beef

*Make a paste of the following 5 ingredients
by adding 3 tbsps water*
1 tsp ground cumin
1½ tsps ground coriander
1 tsp ground fennel
½ tsp ground turmeric
½ tsp garam masala

1 small tin of tomatoes
90ml/3fl oz water
1 fresh green chilli, finely chopped
2 tbsps chopped coriander leaves
1 egg, beaten
2 tbsps milk
2 tbsps flour
100g/4oz golden breadcrumbs
Oil for deep frying

1. Boil the potatoes in their jacket, peel and mash them. Add half the chilli powder and ½ tsp salt from the specified amount. Divide the mixture into 14 golf-ball sized portions, cover and keep aside.

2. Heat the oil over medium heat and fry the fennel seeds until they are brown.

3. Add the onions, ginger and garlic, and stir and fry until the onions are lightly browned (6-8 minutes).

4. Add the mince and fry until all moisture evaporates, stirring frequently (6-8 minutes).

5. Add the spice paste, stir and fry for 5-6 minutes reducing heat towards the last 2-3 minutes.

6. Add the tomatoes, stir and mix, breaking them up with the back of the spoon. Adjust heat to medium and cook for 3-4 minutes stirring frequently.

7. Add the water, the remaining chilli powder and salt, cover and simmer for 15 minutes. Adjust heat to medium, uncover and cook for 4-5 minutes or until the mixture is completely dry but moist. Stir frequently.

8. Stir in the chopped green chilli and the coriander leaves. Cook for 1-2 minutes stirring constantly, remove from heat and allow to cool completely.

9. Mix the beaten egg with the milk and keep aside.

10. Take a portion of the potato and roll it between the palms to make a neat smooth ball. Make a depression in the centre and form into a cup shape. Fill this cavity with the mince leaving approx. ¼-inch round the border. Cover the filling by gently pressing the entire circular border together. Roll between the palms and flatten to form a round cake, about ½-inch thick.

11. Dust the cake in the flour then dip in egg and milk mixture and roll in the breadcrumbs. Make the rest of the patties the same way.

12. Deep fry the patties until they are golden brown. Drain on absorbent paper.

TIME Preparation takes 45-50 minutes, cooking takes 35-40 minutes.

BOTI KABAB

Tender boneless lamb is the traditional meat used for these kababs. They are marinated in a spice-laced yogurt dressing before cooking.

SERVES 6

700g/1½lbs boned leg of lamb
2 small cloves of garlic, peeled and
    chopped
2 tbsps chopped coriander leaves
2 tbsps lemon juice
75g/3oz thick set natural yogurt
Salt to taste
½ tsp ground turmeric
2 tbsps cooking oil

Grind the following 4 ingredients in a coffee grinder:
6 green cardamons (with the skin)
1 cinnamon stick, 1-inch long
2-3 dried red chillies
1 tbsp coriander seeds

To garnish
Thinly sliced onion rings, separated
Crisp lettuce leaves
Wedges of cucumber

---

1. Wash the meat and dry with a cloth.

2. Prick all over with a sharp knife and cut into 1½-inch cubes.

3. Put the garlic, coriander leaves, lemon juice and yogurt into a liquidiser or food processor and blend until smooth. Add the salt, turmeric and the ground ingredients.

4. Put the meat into a bowl and add the liquidised ingredients.

5. Mix thoroughly, cover and leave to marinate for 6-8 hours (or overnight in the refrigerator).

6. Preheat grill to high.

7. Line the grill pan with a piece of aluminium foil (this will reflect heat and also keep your grill pan clean).

8. Thread meat onto skewers leaving about ¼-inch gap between each piece.

9. Mix any remaining marinade with the oil and keep aside.

10. Place the skewers on the prepared grill pan and grill the kababs for 2-3 minutes.

11. Turn the skewers over and grill for a further 2-3 minutes.

12. Reduce heat to medium. Brush the kababs with the oil/marinade mixture and grill for 6-8 minutes.

13. Turn the skewers over and brush the kababs with the remaining oil/marinade mixture. Grill for a further 6-8 minutes.

TIME Preparation takes 20 minutes plus time needed for marinating, cooking takes 15-20 minutes.

SERVING IDEAS Serve as a starter, using ingredients given for garnishing. Serve on cocktail sticks with drinks or as a side dish for a dinner party.

VARIATION Use fillet of pork.

WATCHPOINT Do not overcook the Kababs: follow the cooking time precisely so that the Kababs remain succulent after cooking.

ROTIS

Rotis are a type of unleavened wholemeal bread. The dough is enriched with ghee or butter as for Parathas, but they are much easier to make. If you cannot get chapatti flour, use equal quantities of wholemeal flour and plain flour.

MAKES 8 Rotis

½ tsp salt
50g/2oz butter, or ghee
325g/12oz atta/chapatti flour or 160g/6oz
  each of wholemeal and plain flour
170ml-280ml/6-10fl oz warm water
  (quantity depends on the texture of the
  flour)
2 tbsps ghee or unsalted butter for frying

1. Hand Method: Rub the salt and fat into the flour until you reach a coarse breadcrumb consistency. Gradually add the water and knead until a soft and pliable dough is formed.

2. Food Mixer Method: Put the salt, fat and flour into the bowl and switch on to minimum speed. When the fat has completely broken up and incorporated well into the flour, gradually add the water and knead until the dough is soft and pliable.

3. Divide the dough into 8 balls. Hold each ball between your palms and rotate it in a circular motion until it is smooth and round, flatten the ball into a round cake and dust it very lightly in a little plain flour. Roll it out to about 6-inch diameter; cover the rest of the balls with a damp cloth while you are working on one.

4. Heat a heavy-based frying pan over medium heat; it is important to have a heavy-based pan as the rotis need even distribution of heat.

5. When the pan is hot, place a roti on it and flip it over after about 30 seconds. Spread 1 tsp ghee or butter over it and turn the roti over. Repeat the process for the other side. Brown both sides evenly and remove from heat.

6. Line a piece of aluminium foil with absorbent paper and put the cooked rotis on one end, cover with the other end and seal the edges. This will keep the rotis warm for 30-40 minutes.

TIME Preparation takes 15-30 minutes, cooking takes 25-30 minutes.

SERVING IDEAS Serve with any meat, chicken or vegetable curry.
Suitable for freezing.

PARATHAS

A Paratha is a crisp, rich unleavened bread. The dough is made with a fair amount of fat and each paratha is rolled out, spread with a little ghee or butter, folded and rolled out again to its final shape. It is rather like making flaky pastry but the method is simpler.

MAKES 4 Parathas

325g/12 oz wholemeal flour or chapatti flour (atta) plus 1 tbsp extra flour for dusting
½ tsp salt
125g/5oz ghee or unsalted butter
125-150ml/4-5fl oz warm water

1. Sift the flour and the salt together. Rub 50g/2oz fat from the specified amount into the flour until thoroughly mixed.

2. Gradually pour in the water and knead the mixture until you get a soft and pliable dough.

3. Divide the dough into 4 equal sized balls and flatten them by placing them between your palms and pressing gently.

4. Dust each flattened portion of dough with the flour and roll out to 8-inch diameter. On this spread about one tsp of fat evenly from the remaining 3oz portion.

5. With your hands, roll up the dough from the edge until you have a tube about an inch wide and 8 inches long. Gently stretch the dough lengthways and then curl each end inwards in an anti-clockwise direction to resemble a backwards S.

6. Now flip the upper half onto the lower half and flatten. Lightly dust this all over with flour and roll out again until the dough is about 8-inch diameter and one-eighth-of-an-inch in thickness.

7. Melt remaining fat and keep aside; heat the frying pan (preferably a cast iron one) over medium heat and place the paratha on it. Flip it over in about 30 seconds.

8. Spread 1 tbsp of the melted fat on the paratha. Flip it over again. Lower heat. Spread 1 tbsp of the melted fat on this side as well.

9. With a steel or a wooden spatula press the paratha gently into the frying pan, especially the edges. Flip it over after one minute and repeat the pressing action. Cook the second side for one minute.

10. Continue to cook both sides evenly till the paratha is uniformly light brown.

TIME Preparation takes 30 minutes, cooking takes 20 minutes.

TANDOORI ROTI

Tandoori Rotis are cooked in the Tandoor – a barrel-shaped clay oven which distributes an even and fierce heat. Tandoori rotis can be cooked in a very hot conventional oven, they are equally delicious though the flavour is different.

MAKES 8 Rotis

125g/5oz natural yogurt
450g/1lb plain flour
1 tsp sugar
1 tsp baking powder
½ tsp salt
1½ sachets fast action yeast
1 level tbsp ghee or unsalted butter
1 medium egg, beaten
150ml/5fl oz warm milk

1. Beat the yogurt until smooth, and set aside.

2. In a large bowl, sift the flour with the sugar, baking powder, salt and yeast. Add ghee and mix thoroughly. Add yogurt and egg and knead well, use food mixer or food processor with dough hook, if preferred.

3. Gradually add the warm milk and keep kneading until a smooth and springy dough is formed.

4. Place the dough in a large plastic food bag and tie up the uppermost part of the bag so that the dough has enough room for expansion inside.

5. Rinse a large bowl with hot water and put the bag of dough in it. Use a steel, metal or enamel bowl as these will retain heat better, or use a saucepan if you do not have a suitable bowl. Place the bowl in a warm place (top of the boiler or airing cupboard is ideal) for ½-¾ hour when it will be almost double in volume.

6. Preheat oven to 225°C/450°F/Gas Mark 8.

7. Line a baking sheet with greased greaseproof paper or baking parchment.

8. Divide the dough into 8 equal-sized balls. Place a ball between your palms and flatten by pressing it down.

9. Dust the ball lightly in a little flour and roll it out gently to a 4-inch disc. Place in the prepared baking sheet. Make the rest of the rotis the same way.

10. Bake on the top rung of the oven for 10-12 minutes. Turn the rotis over and bake for a further 2 minutes.

TIME Preparation takes 10-15 minutes, cooking takes 25 minutes.

SERVING IDEAS Serve with any meat, chicken or vegetable curry.
Suitable for freezing.

VARIATION Use wholemeal flour.

PLAIN FRIED RICE

Plain fried rice is enjoyable with many dishes as the mild taste blends in happily with other flavours. The recipe below is perfect when you want to cook something quick, but a little more special than boiled rice.

SERVES 4-6

275g/10oz basmati or other long grain rice, washed and soaked in cold water for ½-1 hour
2 tbsps ghee or 3 tbsps cooking oil
1 tsp fennel seeds
1 tsp salt or to taste
500ml/18fl oz water for basmati rice or 600ml/20fl oz for other long grain rice.

1. Drain the rice and set aside.

2. Heat the oil or ghee over medium heat and fry the fennel seeds until they are brown. Add the rice and salt, stir and fry for 4-5 minutes then lower heat for the last 2-3 minutes of cooking.

3. Add the water and bring to the boil. Cover the pan and simmer for 12 minutes for basmati rice and 15-18 minutes for other long grain rice without lifting the lid.

TIME Preparation takes a few minutes plus time needed to soak the rice, cooking takes 20-25 minutes.

WATCHPOINT There is no need to lift the lid to check the rice during cooking. This will only result in the loss of vital steam which helps to cook the rice leaving each grain beautifully separate.

MATTAR PILAU

An easy to prepare pilau rice which has an attractive look provided by the rich green colour of the garden peas.

SERVES 4-6

275g/10oz basmati rice

75g/3oz ghee or unsalted butter

2 tsp fennel seeds

2-3 dried red chillies

6 whole cloves

2 cinnamon sticks, 2-inches long each, broken up

6 green cardamoms, split open the top of each pod

2 bay leaves, crumpled

1 large onion, finely sliced

150g/6oz frozen garden peas

1 tsp ground turmeric

1¼ tsps salt or to taste

570ml/20fl oz water

1. Wash the rice and soak it in cold water for half an hour. Drain thoroughly.

2. Melt the butter over medium heat and fry the fennel seeds until they are brown.

3. Add the chillies, cloves, cinnamon, cardamom and bay leaves. Stir once and add the onions. Fry until the onions are lightly browned, stirring frequently.

4. Add the rice, peas, turmeric and salt. Stir and fry until the rice is fairly dry (4-5 minutes), lowering heat towards the last 1-2 minutes.

5. Add the water and bring to the boil. Cover the pan and simmer for 12-15 minutes without lifting the lid. Remove the pan from heat and leave it undisturbed for a further 10-15 minutes.

TIME Preparation takes 10 minutes plus time needed to soak the rice, cooking takes 25-30 minutes.

CARROT PILAU

An imaginative way to turn plain boiled rice, left over or freshly cooked, into a colourful and flavoursome pilau which can be served with meat, fish or chicken curry.

SERVES 4-6

275g/10oz basmati rice, washed and soaked in cold water for ½ hour

500ml/18fl oz water

1 tsp salt or to taste

1 tsp butter or ghee

2 tbsps ghee or unsalted butter

1 tsp cumin or caraway seeds

1 medium-sized onion, finely sliced

2 cinnamon sticks, each 2-inches long, broken up

4 green cardamoms, split open the top of each pod

1 tsp garam masala or ground mixed spice

150g/6oz coarsely grated carrots

100g/4oz frozen garden peas

½ tsp salt or to taste

1. Drain the rice thoroughly and put into a saucepan with the water.

2. Bring to the boil, stir in the salt and the butter.

3. Allow to boil steadily for 1 minute.

4. Place the lid on the saucepan and simmer for 12-15 minutes. Do not lift the lid during this time.

5. Remove the pan from heat and keep it covered for a further 10 minutes.

6. Meanwhile, prepare the rest of the ingredients.

7. Melt the ghee or butter over medium heat and fry cumin or caraway until they crackle.

8. Add the onions, cinnamon and cardamom. Fry until the onions are lightly browned (4-5 minutes), stirring frequently.

9. Add the garam masala or ground mixed spice, stir and cook for 30 seconds.

10. Add the carrots, peas and the salt, stir and cook for 1-2 minutes.

11. Now add the rice, stir and mix gently using a metal spoon or a fork as wooden spoon or spatula will squash the grains. Remove the pan from heat.

TIME Preparation takes 10-15 minutes plus time needed to soak the rice, cooking takes 25-30 minutes.

TANDOORI FISH

A firm-fleshed white fish is ideal for this dish; it is not necessary to use an expensive fish. The fish should be handled carefully as most white fish tend to flake during cooking.

SERVES 4

450g/1lb fillet or steak of any white fish
2 cloves garlic, peeled and coarsely
    chopped
¼-inch cube of root ginger, peeled and
    coarsely chopped
½ tsp salt
1 tsp ground cumin
1 tsp ground coriander
½ tsp garam masala
¼-½ tsp chilli powder
¼ tsp Tandoori colour or a few drops of red
    food colouring mixed with 1 tbsp tomato
    purée
Juice of half a lemon
3 tbsps water
2 tbsps cooking oil

Mix the following ingredients
in a small bowl
2 heaped tbsps flour
½ tsp chilli powder
¼ tsp salt

1. Wash the fish and dry on absorbent paper. Cut into 1-inch squares. If using frozen fish, defrost it thoroughly and dry on absorbent paper before cutting it.

2. Add the salt to the ginger and garlic and crush to a smooth pulp.

3. In a small bowl, mix together the ginger/garlic pulp, cumin, coriander, garam masala, chilli powder and Tandoori colour or tomato purée mix. Add the lemon juice and water and mix thoroughly. Keep aside.

4. Heat the oil over medium heat in a non-stick or cast iron frying pan. Dust each piece of fish in the seasoned flour and put in the hot oil in a single layer, leave plenty of room in the pan. Fry for 5 minutes, 2½ minutes each side, and drain on absorbent paper. Now return all the fish to the pan.

5. Hold a sieve over the pan and pour the liquid spice mixture into it. Press with the back of a metal spoon until the mixture in the sieve looks dry and very coarse; discard this mixture.

6. Stir gently and cook over medium heat until the fish is fully coated with the spices and the liquid dries up. Remove from heat.

TIME Preparation takes 15 minutes, cooking takes 15-20 minutes.

SERVING IDEAS Serve garnished with shredded lettuce leaves, sliced cucumber and raw onion rings.
Suitable for freezing.

BENGAL FISH CURRY

The abundance of fish in the Bay of Bengal has enabled the people of this north eastern part of India to develop many delicious dishes using fish. In the recipe below, the fish is cooked entirely in natural yogurt which, with the addition of a little gram flour, gives it an unusual touch.

SERVES 4

700g/1½lbs firm fleshed fish such as river
    trout, grey or red mullet
1 tsp ground turmeric
1¼ tsps salt or to taste
5 tbsps cooking oil
1 large onion, finely chopped
¼-in cube of root ginger – peeled and
    finely chopped or grated
1 tbsp ground coriander
½-1 tsp chilli powder
1 tsp paprika
275g/10oz thick set natural yogurt
4-6 whole fresh green chillies
1-2 cloves of garlic, peeled and crushed
1 tbsp besan (gram or chick pea flour)
2 tbsps chopped coriander leaves
    (optional)

---

1. Clean and wash the fish and pat dry.

2. Cut each fish in to 1½-inch pieces.

3. Gently rub into the fish ¼ tsp turmeric and ¼ tsp salt from the specified amount and put it aside for 15-20 minutes.

4. Meanwhile, heat the oil over medium heat; use a pan wide enough to hold the fish in a single layer and fry onion and ginger until the onions are lightly browned (6-7 minutes), stirring frequently.

5. Add coriander, remaining turmeric, chilli powder and the paprika – adjust heat to low and fry for 1-2 minutes, stirring continuously.

6. Beat the yogurt with a fork until smooth and add to the onion and spice mixture, adjust heat to medium, add the whole green chillies, the remaining salt and the garlic. Stir and mix well.

7. Arrange the pieces of fish in this liquid in a single layer and bring to the boil. Cover and cook over low heat for 5-6 minutes.

8. Blend the besan with a little water to make a pouring consistency. Strain this over the fish curry, stir gently, and mix. Cover and cook for 2-3 minutes.

9. Remove from heat and gently mix in half the coriander leaves.

10. Transfer the fish curry into a serving dish and garnish with the remaining coriander leaves (if used).

TIME Preparation takes 20-25 minutes, cooking takes 20 minutes.

SPICED SARDINES

Fresh sardines are easily available from early summer to late autumn. The preparation below is simple and tastes excellent.

SERVES 4

8 fresh sardines (about 700g/1½lb)
1 tsp salt or to taste
3-4 cloves garlic, peeled and coarsely
     chopped
The juice of half a lemon
½ tsp ground turmeric
½-1 tsp chilli powder
3 heaped tbsps plain flour
60ml/2½fl oz cooking oil

1. Scale and clean the fish. Wash gently in cold water and dry on absorbent paper.

2. Add the salt to the garlic and crush to a smooth pulp.

3. Mix all the ingredients together, except the fish, flour and oil, in a small bowl.

4. Put the fish in a wide shallow dish and pour the marinade over. Spread it gently on both sides of the fish, cover and refrigerate for 2-4 hours.

5. Heat the oil over medium heat. Dip each fish in the flour and coat it thoroughly. Fry until golden brown on both sides (2-3 minutes each side). Drain on absorbent paper.

TIME Preparation takes 20 minutes plus 2-4 hours to marinate, cooking takes 6-8 minutes

EGG & POTATO DUM

*Hard-boiled curried eggs are very popular in the northeastern part of India. Here,
the eggs are cooked with potatoes and they are both fried first until they form a
light crust. Slow cooking, without any loss of steam, is the secret of the success of
this dish.*

SERVES 4-6

6 hard-boiled eggs

5 tbsps cooking oil

450g/1lb medium-sized potatoes, peeled
    and quartered

⅛ tsp each of chilli powder and ground
    turmeric, mixed together

1 large onion, finely chopped

½-inch cube of root ginger, peeled and
    grated

1 cinnamon stick, 2-inch long; broken up
    into 2-3 pieces

2 black cardamoms, split open the top of
    each pod

4 whole cloves

1 fresh green chilli, chopped

1 small tin of tomatoes

½ tsp ground turmeric

2 tsps ground coriander

1 tsp ground fennel

¼-½ tsp chilli powder (optional)

1 tsp salt or to taste

225ml/8fl oz warm water

1 tbsp chopped coriander leaves

1. Shell the eggs and make 4 slits
lengthwise on each egg leaving about
½-inch gap on either end.

2. Heat the oil over medium heat in a cast
iron or non-stick pan (enamel or steel pans
will cause the eggs and the potatoes to
stick). Fry the potatoes until they are well
browned on all sides (about 10 minutes).
Remove them with a slotted spoon and
keep aside.

3. Remove the pan from heat and stir in the
turmeric and chilli mixture. Place the pan
back on heat and fry the whole eggs until
they are well browned. Remove them with a
slotted spoon and keep aside.

4. In the same oil, fry the onions, ginger,
cinnamon, cardamom, cloves and green
chilli until the onions are lightly browned
(6-7 minutes).

5. Add half the tomatoes, stir and fry until
the tomatoes break up (2-3 minutes).

6. Add the turmeric, ground coriander,
fennel and chilli powder (if used); stir and
fry for 3-4 minutes.

7. Add the rest of the tomatoes and fry for
4-5 minutes, stirring frequently.

8. Add the potatoes, salt and water, bring to
the boil, cover the pan tightly and simmer
until the potatoes are tender, stirring
occasionally.

9. Now add the eggs and simmer,
uncovered for 5-6 minutes, stirring once or
twice.

10. Stir in the coriander leaves and remove
from heat.

TIME Preparation takes 15 minutes, cooking takes 35-40 minutes.

TANDOORI CHICKEN

The Tandoor, because of its fierce but even distribution of heat, enables meat to cook quickly, forming a light crust on the outside but leaving the inside moist and succulent.
It is possible to achieve perfectly satisfactory results by using a conventional gas or electric oven at the highest temperature setting, though the distinctive flavour of clay-cooked chicken will not be achieved.

SERVES 4-6

1.2kg/2½lbs chicken joints, legs or breast or
    a combination of the two
1 tsp salt or to taste
Juice of half a lemon
½-inch cube of root ginger, peeled and
    coarsely chopped
2-3 small cloves of garlic, peeled and
    coarsely chopped
1 fresh green chilli, coarsely chopped and
    seeded if a milder flavour is required
2 tbsps chopped coriander leaves
75g/3oz thick set natural yogurt
1 tsp ground coriander
½ tsp ground cumin
1 tsp garam masala
¼ tsp freshly ground black pepper
½ tsp Tandoori colour (available from
    Indian grocers in powder form), or a few
    drops of red food colouring mixed with
    1 tbsp tomato purée

1. Remove skin from the chicken and cut each piece into two. With a sharp knife, make 2-3 slits in each piece. Rub salt and lemon juice into the chicken pieces and set aside for half an hour.

2. Meanwhile, put the ginger, garlic, green chillies, coriander leaves and the yogurt into a liquidiser and blend until smooth. Add the rest of the ingredients and blend again.

3. Pour and spread the marinade all over the chicken, especially into the slits. Cover the container with cling film and leave to marinate for 6-8 hours or overnight in the refrigerator.

4. Preheat oven to 240°C/475°F/Gas Mark 9. Line a roasting tin with aluminium foil (this will help to maintain the high level of heat required to cook the chicken) and arrange the chicken pieces in it. Place the roasting tin in the centre of the oven and bake for 25-30 minutes, turning the pieces over carefully as they brown and basting with juice in the roasting tin as well as any remaining marinade.

5. Remove from the oven, lift each piece with a pair of tongs and shake off any excess liquid.

TIME Preparation takes 20-25 minutes, cooking takes 25-30 minutes.

MURGH DILKUSH

Chicken is still regarded as a bit special in India as it is more expensive than other meats. This is a wonderfully aromatic chicken dish which is ideally suited for a special occasion.

SERVES 6-8

1.2kg/2½lbs chicken joints, skin removed

4 tbsps ghee or unsalted butter

2 medium-sized onions, finely chopped

1-inch cube of root ginger, peeled and coarsely chopped

4-6 cloves garlic, peeled and coarsely chopped

125g/5oz thick set natural yogurt

Roast the following ingredients gently over low heat until the spices release their aroma, cool and grind in a coffee grinder.

2-inch piece cinnamon stick, broken up

6 green cardamoms, skin left on

6 whole cloves

1 tsp cumin seeds

2-3 dried red chillies

1 tbsp channa dhal or yellow split peas

Similarly, roast the following 2 ingredients until they are lightly browned, cool and grind separately from the above ingredients, in a coffee grinder.

25g/1oz raw cashews

1 tbsp white poppy seeds

1 tsp garam masala

150ml/5fl oz warm water

1¼ tsps salt or to taste

25g/1 oz fresh coriander leaves, finely chopped

1 tbsp fresh mint leaves, finely chopped or 1 tsp dried or bottled mint

1-2 fresh green chillies, seeded and coarsely chopped

1. Cut each chicken joint into two (separate leg from thigh and cut each breast into two).

2. Melt 2 tbsps ghee, from the specified amount, over medium heat and fry the onions, ginger and garlic for 4-5 minutes. Squeeze out excess ghee by pressing the onion mixture onto the side of the pan with a wooden spoon and transfer them to another plate. Allow to cool slightly.

3. Put the yogurt into an electric blender or food processor and add all the roasted and ground ingredients and the fried onions. Blend until smooth.

4. Rub this marinade into the chicken and pour over any remaining marinade – mix thoroughly and leave to marinate for 4-6 hours or overnight in the refrigerator.

5. Melt the remaining 2 tbsps ghee over low heat and add the garam masala, stir and fry for 30 seconds.

6. Add the marinated chicken, adjust heat to medium-high and fry for 5-6 minutes, stirring frequently.

7. Add the water and salt, bring to the boil, cover and simmer until the chicken is tender (35-40 minutes).

8. Adjust heat to medium, add the fresh coriander, mint and green chillies – stir and fry for 5 minutes and remove from heat.

CHICKEN WITH WHOLE SPICES

This recipe is the answer to a good, tasty curry in a hurry! With this curry on the menu, you can present a whole meal in approximately one hour.

SERVES 4-6

1kg/2.2lbs chicken joints, skinned

4 tbsps cooking oil

1 tsp cumin seeds

1 large onion, finely chopped

½-inch cube of root ginger, peeled and finely chopped

2-4 cloves garlic, peeled and crushed or finely chopped

2-3 dried red chillies, whole

2 cinnamon sticks, 2-inches long each, broken up

2 black cardamoms, split open the top of each pod

4 whole cloves

10 whole allspice seeds

½ tsp ground turmeric

1 tsp paprika

150ml/5fl oz warm water

1¼ tsp salt or to taste

2 ripe tomatoes, skinned and chopped

2 fresh green chillies, whole

1 tbsp ground almond

2 tbsps chopped coriander leaves (optional)

1. Cut each chicken joint in two; separate leg from thigh and cut each breast in two.

2. Heat the oil over medium heat and fry the cumin seeds until they pop, then add the onions, ginger, garlic and red chillies. Fry until the onions are soft but not brown, stirring frequently.

3. Add the cinnamon, cardamom, cloves and allspice, stir and fry for 30 seconds.

4. Stir in the turmeric and paprika and immediately follow with the chicken. Adjust heat to medium-high and fry the chicken until it changes colour (5-6 minutes), stirring frequently.

5. Add the water and salt, bring to the boil, cover the pan and simmer until the chicken is tender (about 30 minutes).

6. Add the tomatoes, green chillies and the ground almonds. Stir and mix well, cover the pan and simmer for a further 6-8 minutes.

7. Stir in half the coriander leaves and remove the pan from heat.

8. Transfer the chicken into a serving dish and garnish with the remaining coriander leaves, (if used).

TIME Preparation takes 15-20 minutes, cooking takes 50 minutes.

CHICKEN LIVER MASALA

*Curried liver is quite a popular item in India, particularly with Muslims.
This recipe is made more interesting by adding diced potatoes and
frozen garden peas.*

SERVES 4

450g/1lb chicken liver
4 tbsps cooking oil
1 large onion finely chopped
1 cinnamon stick, 2-inches long, broken up
225g/8oz potatoes, peeled and diced
1¼ tsps salt or to taste
90ml/3fl oz warm water
3-4 cloves garlic, peeled and crushed

*Make a paste of the following 4 ingredients
by adding 2 tsps water*
2 tsps ground coriander
1 tsp ground cumin
1 tsp ground turmeric
½ tsp chilli powder

1 small tin of tomatoes
100g/4oz frozen garden peas
2-3 fresh green chillies, whole
½ tsp garam masala

---

1. Clean the liver, remove all skin and gristle and cut roughly into ½-inch pieces.

2. Heat 2 tbsps oil over medium heat and fry the onions and cinnamon stick until the onions are soft.

3. Add the potatoes and ¼ tsp salt and stir fry the potatoes for about 2 minutes.

4. Add the water, cover the pan and simmer until the potatoes are tender.

5. Meanwhile, heat the remaining oil over medium heat in a heavy-based, wide pan. A nonstick or cast iron pan is ideal as the liver needs to be stir-fried over high heat.

6. Add the garlic and stir fry for 30 seconds.

7. Add the spice paste, reduce heat to low, and stir and fry for about 2 minutes.

8. Add half the tomatoes, along with some of the juice, stir and cook for a further 2-3 minutes, breaking the tomatoes with the spoon.

9. When the mixture is fairly dry, add the liver and adjust heat to medium-high. Stir-fry the liver for 3-4 minutes.

10. Add the remaining tomatoes and the juice, stir and fry for 5-6 minutes.

11. Cover the pan and simmer for 6-8 minutes.

12. Add the potatoes, peas, green chillies and the remaining salt and cook for 1-2 minutes. Adjust heat to medium and cook, uncovered, for a further 4-5 minutes.

13. Stir in the garam masala and remove from heat.

TIME Preparation takes 20-25 minutes, cooking takes 36-40 minutes.

MURGHI AUR PALAK

Murghi aur Palak is a delicious combination of chicken and spinach with fennel, coriander and chillies.

SERVES 4-6

1kg/2.2lbs chicken quarters, skinned
4 tbsps cooking oil
2 medium-sized onions, finely chopped
1-inch cube of root ginger, peeled and
    finely grated
2-3 cloves garlic, peeled and crushed

*Make a paste of the following 4 ingredients
by adding 3 tbsps water*
1 tsp ground turmeric
1 tsp ground fennel
1 tsp ground coriander
½ tsp chilli powder

1½ tsps salt or to taste
90ml/3fl oz warm water
1 heaped tbsp ghee or unsalted butter
1-2 cloves garlic, peeled and finely
    chopped
6-8 curry leaves
½ tsp cumin seeds
½ tsp fennel seeds
1-2 dried red chillies, coarsely chopped
450g/1lb fresh or 225g/8oz frozen leaf
    spinach, (defrosted and drained)
    coarsely chopped
4 tbsps natural yogurt
½ tsp garam masala

1. Cut each chicken quarter into half, separating leg from thigh and cutting each breast into two, lengthwise.

2. Heat the oil over medium heat and fry the onions, ginger and garlic until the onions are lightly browned (6-8 minutes).

3. Adjust heat to low and add the spice paste, stir and fry for 4-5 minutes. Rinse out the bowl with 2 tbsps water and add to the spice mixture. Stir and fry for a further 2-3 minutes.

4. Add the chicken and adjust heat to medium-high. Stir and fry until chicken changes colour (about 3-4 minutes). Add 1 tsp salt and the water, bring to the boil, cover the pan and simmer for 15 minutes; stir once or twice during this time.

5. In a separate pan, melt ghee or butter over medium heat and add garlic and curry leaves followed by cumin, fennel and red chillies, stirring briskly. Wash fresh spinach thoroughly, remove any hard stalks and add the spinach and the remaining salt. Stir and fry for 5-6 minutes and mix spinach and chicken together, bring to the boil, cover the pan and simmer for 20 minutes, stirring occasionally.

6. Mix yogurt and garam masala together and beat until the yogurt is smooth. Add to the chicken/spinach mixture – stir and mix thoroughly. Cook uncovered for 6-8 minutes over medium heat, stirring frequently.

TIME Preparation takes 25-30 minutes, cooking takes 50-55 minutes.

CHICKEN KOHLAPURI

This delicious chicken dish comes from Kohlapur in southern India. The original recipe has a large amount of chillies as people in this part of India prefer a very hot flavour. For this recipe, however, the quantity of chillies has been reduced.

SERVES 4-6

1.4kg/2½lbs chicken joints, skinned

1 large onion, coarsely chopped

3-4 cloves garlic, peeled and coarsely chopped

1-inch cube of root ginger, peeled and coarsely chopped

6 tbsps cooking oil

1 tsp ground turmeric

2 tsps ground coriander

1½ tsps ground cumin

1-1¼ tsps chilli powder

1 small tin of tomatoes

1¼ tsps salt or to taste

180ml/6fl oz water

4-6 whole green chillies

1 tsp garam masala

2 tbsps chopped coriander leaves

1. Cut each chicken joint in two (separate legs from thighs or cut breast into 2-3 pieces); wash and dry on absorbent paper.

2. Place the onion, garlic and ginger in an electric food processor or liquidiser and blend to a smooth purée. You may need to add a little water if you are using a liquidiser.

3. Heat the oil over medium heat and add the liquidised ingredients. Stir and fry for 5-6 minutes.

4. Add turmeric, ground coriander, cumin and chilli powder; adjust heat to low and fry for 4-5 minutes stirring frequently.

5. Add half the tomatoes, stir and cook for 2-3 minutes.

6. Now add the chicken, stir and cook until chicken changes colour (4-5 minutes) and add the rest of the tomatoes, along with all the juice.

7. Add salt and water, bring to the boil, cover and simmer until the chicken is tender. Stir occasionally to ensure that the thickened gravy does not stick to the bottom of the pan.

8. Add the whole green chillies and garam masala, cover and simmer for 5 minutes.

9. Remove the pan from heat and stir in the coriander leaves.

TIME Preparation takes 15-20 minutes, cooking takes 55 minutes.

WATCHPOINT In stage 3, it is important to fry the ingredients for the specified time so that the raw smell of the onions, ginger and garlic can be eliminated before adding the rest of the ingredients.

MURGHI NAWABI

This is a classic example of the popular Mughal cuisine which is noted for its delicate flavourings and rich smooth sauces. The chicken is marinated in yogurt and turmeric and simmered in delicately flavoured coconut milk.

SERVES 4-6

1kg/2.2lbs chicken joints, skinned

125g/5oz thick set natural yogurt

½ tsp ground turmeric

3-4 cloves garlic, peeled and coarsely chopped

1-inch cube of root ginger, peeled and coarsely chopped

4-6 dried red chillies

50g/2oz ghee or unsalted butter

2 large onions, finely sliced

1 tsp caraway seeds

1 tsp garam masala

1¼ tsps salt or to taste

225ml/8fl oz warm water plus 90ml/3fl oz cold water

85g/3½oz creamed coconut, cut into small pieces

75g/3oz raw cashews

2 hard-boiled eggs, sliced

¼ tsp paprika

1. Cut each chicken joint into two pieces (separate leg from thigh and cut each breast into two pieces). Wash the chicken and dry on absorbent paper.

2. Beat the yogurt and turmeric powder together until smooth. Add to the chicken and mix thoroughly, cover the container and leave to marinate for 4-6 hours or overnight in the refrigerator.

3. Put the garlic, ginger and red chillies in an electric liquidiser and add just enough water to facilitate blade movement and mixing. Blend until the ingredients are smooth. Alternatively, crush the garlic, ginger and finely chop the chillies.

4. Melt the ghee or butter over medium heat and fry the onions until they are brown (8-10 minutes). Remove the pan from heat and, using a wooden spatula, press the onions to the side of the pan in order to squeeze out excess fat. Transfer the onions onto a plate and keep aside.

5. Place the pan back on heat and fry the caraway seeds and garam masala for 30 seconds. Add the blended ingredients. Stir briskly and add the chicken, fried onions and salt. Fry the chicken for 5-6 minutes, stirring frequently and lowering heat as the chicken is heated through. If there is any yogurt marinade left in the container add this to the chicken.

6. Add the water and the creamed coconut. Bring to the boil, cover the pan and simmer until the chicken is tender and the gravy is thick (30-35 minutes). Stir occasionally during this time.

7. Meanwhile, put the cashews into an electric blender and add the cold water and blend until smooth. Add the cashew paste to the chicken during the last 5 minutes of cooking time. Simmer uncovered for 4-5 minutes, stirring frequently.

8. Put the chicken into a serving dish and garnish with the sliced eggs. Sprinkle the paprika on top.

CORIANDER CHICKEN

Coriander Chicken is quick and easy to make, it tastes wonderful and looks very impressive – a perfect choice for any dinner party menu.

SERVES 4-6

1kg/2.2lbs chicken joints, skinned
2-4 cloves garlic, peeled and crushed
125g/5oz thick set natural yogurt
5 tbsps cooking oil
1 large onion, finely sliced
2 tbsps ground coriander
½ tsp ground black pepper
1 tsp ground mixed spice
½ tsp ground turmeric
½ tsp cayenne pepper or chilli powder
125ml/4fl oz warm water
1 tsp salt or to taste
25g/1oz ground almonds
2 hard-boiled eggs, sliced
¼ tsp paprika

1. Cut each chicken joint into two, mix thoroughly with the crushed garlic and the yogurt. Cover the container and leave to marinate in a cool place for 2-4 hours or overnight in the refrigerator.

2. Heat the oil over medium heat and fry the onions until they are golden brown (6-8 minutes). Remove with a slotted spoon and keep aside.

3. In the same oil, fry the coriander, ground pepper, ground mixed spice and turmeric for 15 seconds and add the chicken along with all the marinade in the container.

4. Adjust heat to medium-high and fry the chicken until it changes colour (5-6 minutes).

5. Add the cayenne or chilli powder, water, salt, and the fried onion slices. Bring to the boil, cover the pan and simmer until the chicken is tender (about 30 minutes).

6. Stir in the ground almonds and remove from heat.

TIME Preparation takes 20 minutes plus time needed for marinating, cooking takes 45-50 minutes.

WATCHPOINT Reduce cooking time if boneless chicken is used.

MURGH MUSALLAM

SERVES 4-6

2 spring chickens or poussin, each
  weighing about 450g/1lb

Grind together the following 5 ingredients
2 tbsps white poppy seeds
2 tbsps sesame seeds
10 black peppercorns
4 green cardamoms
2-4 dried red chillies

125g/5oz thick set natural yogurt
2½ tsps salt or to taste
½ tsp ground turmeric
1 tbsp ground coriander
75g/3oz ghee or unsalted butter
2 medium-sized onions, finely sliced
2-3 cloves garlic, peeled and finely
  chopped
2 cinnamon sticks, 2-inches each;
  broken up
6 green cardamoms, split open the top of
  each pod
4 whole cloves
275g/10oz basmati rice, washed and soaked
  in cold water for 30 minutes
570ml/20fl oz water
½ tsp saffron strands
2 tbsps ghee or unsalted butter
1 medium-sized onion, finely chopped
2-4 cloves garlic, peeled and crushed

1. Remove the skin and the giblets from the chicken. With a sharp knife, make several slits all over each chicken (do not forget the thighs and the back).
2. Mix the ground ingredients with the yogurt and add 1 tsp salt, turmeric and coriander. Rub half of this mixture into the chickens, making sure that the spices are rubbed deep into the slits. Put the chickens in a deep container, cover and keep aside for 1 hour.

3. Meanwhile cook the pilau rice. Melt the 75g/3oz ghee or butter over medium heat and fry the sliced onions, chopped garlic, cinnamon, cardamom and cloves, until the onions are lightly browned (6-7 minutes).
4. Add the rice, stir and fry until all the moisture evaporates (4-5 minutes). Add the remaining salt, water and saffron strands. Bring to the boil, cover the pan and simmer until the rice has absorbed all the water (12-14 minutes). Do not lift the lid or stir the rice during cooking. Remove the pan from the heat and leave it undisturbed for about 10 minutes.
5. Using a metal spoon, carefully transfer about a quarter of the cooked rice to a plate and allow it to cool. Keep the remaining rice covered.
6. Stuff each chicken with as much of the cooled pilau rice as the stomach cavity will hold. Truss it up as for roasting, using trussing needles or a similar object to secure it so that the rice stays in tact while the stuffed chicken is being braised.
7. Melt the 2 tbsps ghee or butter in a cast iron or nonstick pan. Add the chopped onions and the crushed garlic, stir and fry for 2-3 minutes.
8. Place the chicken on the bed of onions, on their backs, along with any marinade left in the container, but not the other half of the marinade which has been reserved. Cover the pan and cook for 10 minutes; turn the chicken over, breast side down, cover and cook for a further 10 minutes.
9. Turn the chickens on their backs again and spread the remaining marinade evenly on each chicken. Cover the pan and cook for 30 minutes turning the chicken over every 10 minutes.

10. Put the chicken onto a serving dish and spread a little gravy evenly over the breast. Spoon the remaining gravy round the chicken.
11. Serve the remaining pilau rice separately.

KOFTA (MEATBALL) CURRY

*Koftas are popular throughout India, and they are made using fine lean mince
which is blended with herbs and spices.*

SERVES 4

For the koftas
450g/1lb lean minced lamb
2 cloves garlic, peeled and chopped
½-inch cube of root ginger, peeled and
    coarsely chopped
1 small onion, coarsely chopped
55ml/2fl oz water
1 fresh green chilli, seeded and chopped
2 tbsps chopped coriander leaves
1 tbsp fresh mint leaves, chopped
1 tsp salt or to taste

For the gravy
5 tbsps cooking oil
2 medium-sized onions, finely chopped
½-inch cube of root ginger, peeled and
    grated
2 cloves garlic, peeled and crushed
2 tsps ground coriander
1½ tsps ground cumin
½ tsp ground turmeric
¼-½ tsp chilli powder
1 small tin of tomatoes
150ml/5fl oz warm water
½ tsp salt or to taste
2 black cardamom pods, opened
4 whole cloves
2-inch piece of cinnamon stick, broken up
2 bay leaves, crumpled
2 tbsps thick set natural yogurt
2 tbsps ground almonds
1 tbsp chopped coriander leaves

1. Put half the mince, all the garlic, ginger,
onion and the water into a saucepan and
place over medium heat. Stir until the
mince is heated through.

2. Cover and simmer until all liquid
evaporates (30-35 minutes) then cook
uncovered if necessary, to dry out excess
liquid.

3. Combine the cooked mince with the rest
of the ingredients, including the raw mince.

4. Put the mixture into a food processor or
liquidiser and blend until smooth. Chill the
mixture for 30 minutes.

5. Divide the mixture into approximately 20
balls, each slightly bigger than a walnut.

6. Rotate each ball between your palms to
make neat round koftas.

7. Heat the oil over medium heat and fry
the onions until they are just soft.

8. Add the ginger and garlic and fry for 1
minute.

9. Add the coriander, cumin, turmeric and
chilli powder and stir quickly.

10. Add one tomato at a time, along with a
little juice to the spice mixture, stirring until
mixture begins to look dry.

11. Now add the water, salt, cardamom,
cloves, cinnamon and the bay leaves.

12. Stir once and add the koftas. Bring to
the boil, cover and simmer for 5 minutes.

13. Beat the yogurt with a fork until smooth,
add the ground almonds and beat again –
stir GENTLY into the curry. Cover and
simmer until the koftas are firm.

14. Stir the curry GENTLY, cover again, and
simmer for a further 10-15 minutes, stirring
occasionally to ensure that the thickened
gravy does not stick to the pan.

15. Stir in half the coriander leaves and
remove from heat.

Cauliflower Surprise

Here is an imaginative way to serve cauliflower which also looks attractive. The cauliflower is first blanched, then stuffed with spicy lean mince.

SERVES 4

1 medium-sized cauliflower

4 tbsps cooking oil

1 tsp cumin seeds

1 large onion, finely chopped

1-inch cube of root ginger, peeled and grated

3-4 cloves garlic, peeled and crushed

450g/1lb lean mince, lamb or beef

1 tsp ground turmeric

1 tbsp ground coriander

1 tsp ground cinnamon

1 tsp ground cardamom

½ tsp chilli powder

1 small tin of tomatoes, drained

1 tsp salt or to taste

¼ tsp black mustard seeds

½ tsp cumin seeds

8-10 curry leaves

To garnish

2 small tomatoes, quartered

1 tbsp chopped coriander leaves

1. Blanch the cauliflower in boiling salted water, then drain and cool.

2. Heat 3 tbsps oil over medium heat and add the cumin seeds; as soon as the seeds start popping, add the onions and fry for 3-4 minutes, stirring frequently.

3. Add the ginger and garlic, stir and fry for 1 minute.

4. Add the mince, adjust heat to medium-high, stir and fry the mince until it is crumbly and all the liquid evaporates.

5. Adjust heat to low and add the turmeric, coriander, cinnamon, cardamom and chilli powder. Stir and fry until the spices are well-blended (3-4 minutes).

6. Add the tomatoes and salt, stir and cook for 1-2 minutes. Cover the pan and simmer for 10-15 minutes. Remove the pan from heat and allow the mince to cool.

7. Place the cauliflower on a board, stem side up. Fill all the cavity between the stems with the cooked mince; this should be as tightly packed as possible.

8. Turn the cauliflower over and gently pull the florets apart and fill with as much mince as possible.

9. Heat the remaining oil over medium heat and add the mustard seeds. As soon as the seeds pop, add the cumin and the curry leaves.

10. Place the cauliflower on the seasoned oil, the right way up, and let it cook, uncovered for 2-3 minutes. Turn it over and cook the other side for 2-3 minutes.

11. Turn the cauliflower over again and arrange the remaining mince round it. Cover the pan and adjust heat to the minimum setting. Cook for 10-15 minutes or until the cauliflower is tender.

12. Put the cauliflower on a serving dish and spread some of the mince on it and arrange any remaining mince round it. Garnish with the tomatoes and the coriander leaves.

TIME Preparation takes 20 minutes plus cooling time, cooking takes 55-60 minutes.

BHOONA GOSHT

*The word 'Bhoon' means to fry and 'Gosht' means meat; Bhoona Gosht,
therefore, means fried meat. This dish needs particular care and attention
during frying. It is important to follow carefully the different level of temperature
during the different stages of frying.*

SERVES 4-6

1kg/2.2lbs leg or shoulder of lamb

5 tbsps cooking oil

3 large onions, finely chopped

1-inch cube of root ginger, peeled and
    grated or finely chopped

3-4 cloves garlic, peeled and crushed

1 tsp ground turmeric

2 tsps ground cumin

1 tbsp ground coriander

½-1 tsp chilli powder

200ml/7fl oz warm water

1¼ tsps salt or to taste

2 medium-sized ripe tomatoes, skinned and
    chopped; tinned tomatoes can be used

4-5 whole fresh green chillies

1 tsp garam masala

1 tbsps chopped coriander leaves

2 small ripe tomatoes, sliced

1. Trim off excess fat from the meat, wash
and cut into 1-inch cubes. Drain on
absorbent paper.

2. Heat the oil over medium heat and add
the onions, ginger and garlic. Fry until the
onions are just soft (about 5 minutes).

3. Lower heat and add the turmeric, cumin,
coriander and chilli powder. Stir and fry for
2-3 minutes.

4. Add the meat, turn heat to medium and
fry for 5 minutes stirring frequently. Cover
the pan and cook on medium heat until all
the liquid dries out (15-20 minutes). Stir
frequently.

5. Turn heat to high and fry the meat for 2-3
minutes stirring continuously. Reduce heat
to medium and fry for a further 7-8 minutes
stirring frequently. The meat should now
look fairly dry and the fat should be floating
on the surface. Some of the fat can be
drained off at this stage, but be careful not
to drain off any of the spices.

6. Add the water and salt, bring to the boil,
cover and simmer for 50-60 minutes or until
the meat is tender. Add more water if
necessary. At the end of the cooking time,
the thick spice paste should be clinging to
the pieces of meat.

7. Add the chopped tomatoes and the
whole green chillies. Stir and fry for 3-4
minutes.

8. Stir in the garam masala and half the
coriander leaves and remove from heat.

9. Put the bhoona gosht into a serving dish
and arrange the sliced tomatoes round the
meat. Sprinkle the remaining coriander
leaves on top.

TIME Preparation takes 25-30 minutes, cooking takes 1 hour 45 minutes.

MEAT DILPASAND

A delectable lamb dish with a slightly creamy texture and a wonderfully nutty flavour derived from roasted and ground poppy seeds.

SERVES 4-6

1kg/2.2lbs leg of lamb
125g/5oz thick set natural yogurt
1 tsp ground turmeric
2 tbsps white poppy seeds
1-inch cube of root ginger, peeled and coarsely chopped
4-5 cloves garlic, peeled and coarsely chopped
1-2 fresh green chillies, seed them if a milder flavour is preferred
450g/1lb onions
3 tbsps ghee or unsalted butter
½ tsp chilli powder
1 tsp paprika
1 tbsp ground cumin
1 tsp garam masala
1 tbsp tomato purée
1¼ tsps salt or to taste
175ml/6fl oz warm water
25g/1oz creamed coconut or 2 tbsps desiccated coconut
2 tbsps chopped coriander leaves

---

1. Trim off any fat from the meat, wash and dry on absorbent paper and cut into 1½-inch cubes.

2. Add yogurt and turmeric, mix thoroughly, cover the container and leave to marinate for 4-6 hours or overnight in the refrigerator.

3. Roast the poppy seeds without fat over gentle heat until they are a shade darker – allow to cool.

4. Place the ginger, garlic and green chillies in an electric blender or food processor. Chop one onion, from the specified amount, and add to the ginger and garlic

mixture. Blend until fairly smooth.

5. Chop the remaining onions finely.

6. Melt the ghee or butter over medium heat and fry onions until golden brown. This will take 10 to 12 minutes.

7. Adjust heat to low and add chilli powder, paprika, cumin and ½ tsp garam masala from the specified amount. Stir and fry for 2-3 minutes.

8. Now add the liquidised ingredients and fry for 10 to 12 minutes, stirring frequently. If during this time the spices tend to stick to the bottom of the pan, sprinkle with about 1 tbsp of water at a time as and when necessary.

9. Add the meat and adjust heat to medium-high. Fry for 4-5 minutes stirring constantly.

10. Add the tomato purée, salt and water, stir and mix, bring to the boil, cover and simmer for 45 minutes or until the meat is tender. Stir occasionally during the first half of cooking, but more frequently towards the end to ensure that the thickened gravy does not stick to the bottom of the pan.

11. If you are using creamed coconut, cut into small pieces with a sharp knife. Desiccated coconut should be ground in the coffee grinder before use to ensure that the necessary fine texture is achieved in making the curry. Finish off the cooking process in the same way as for creamed coconut.

12. Grind the poppy seeds in a coffee grinder and stir into the meat along with the creamed coconut. Stir until coconut is dissolved. Cover and simmer for 15 minutes.

13. Stir in the coriander leaves and the remaining garam masala. Remove from heat.

LAMB WITH MUNG BEANS

Mung beans are available from Indian grocers and health food shops. Do prepare this dish a day in advance because the flavour improves significantly when it is left to stand.

SERVES 6-8

150g/6oz whole mung beans

1¼ tsp salt or to taste

1-inch cube of root ginger, peeled and coarsely chopped

2-4 cloves garlic, peeled and coarsely chopped

700g/1½lbs leg or shoulder of lamb, cut into 1-inch cubes

450ml/15fl oz water

1 large onion, finely chopped

Grind the 6 following ingredients in a coffee grinder

2 dried red chillies

1½ tsps cumin seeds

2 tsps coriander seeds

4 whole cloves

1 cinnamon stick, 2-inches long; broken up

4 black peppercorns

1 tsp ground turmeric

1 small tin of tomatoes or 4 ripe tomatoes, skinned and chopped

2 tbsps chopped coriander leaves

1. Soak the mung beans overnight in plenty of cold water and drain well. Pulses usually contain a certain amount of grit and sand; make sure you clean the beans and wash them several times before soaking.

2. Add the salt to the ginger and garlic and crush them to a smooth pulp.

3. Place the meat and water in a large pan and bring the liquid to the boil. Cover the pan and simmer for 45 minutes.

4. Add the mung beans along with the onions. Bring back to the boil, cover the pan and cook on low heat for 25 minutes.

5. Add the ginger/garlic pulp, the ground spices, turmeric and the tomatoes. Simmer for 10 minutes, uncovered.

6. Remove from heat and stand aside for several hours before serving. The longer you let it stand, the better.

7. Reheat the curry and stir in the coriander leaves and simmer for 5 minutes before serving.

TIME Preparation takes 15-20 minutes plus time needed to soak the beans, cooking takes 1 hour 20 minutes.

SERVING IDEAS Serve with Plain Boiled Rice and Tomato and Cucumber Salad.
Suitable for freezing.

VARIATION Add 100g/4oz aubergines, cut into chunky pieces, along with the mung beans.

KHEEMA SHAHZADA

Kheema, or mince is not at all an under-rated item in Indian cookery and in fact, the recipe below elevates mince to gourmet status. Do make sure that the mince is lean and that it is not too fine.

SERVES 4

4 heaped tbsps ghee or unsalted butter

1 large onion, coarsely chopped

1-inch cube of root ginger, peeled and
   coarsely chopped

2-4 cloves garlic, peeled and coarsely
   chopped

*Grind the following ingredients
in a coffee grinder*

1 cinnamon stick, 2-inches long; broken up

4 green cardamoms

4 whole cloves

4-6 dried red chillies

1 tbsp coriander seeds

*Grind the following 2 ingredients
separately*

1 tbsp white poppy seeds

1 tbsp sesame seeds

450g/1lb lean coarse mince

½ tsp ground turmeric

50g/2oz raw cashews, split into halves

1 tsp salt or to taste

300ml/10fl oz warm water

150ml/5fl oz milk

2 hard-boiled eggs, quartered lengthwise

A few sprigs of fresh coriander

1. Melt 2 tbsps ghee or butter from the specified amount, over medium heat and fry the onions, ginger and garlic until the onions are soft (about 5 minutes). Squeeze out excess fat by pressing the fried ingredients onto the side of the pan with a wooden spatula and transfer them to a plate. Allow to cool.

2. Add the remaining ghee or butter to the pan and fry the ground ingredients, including the poppy and sesame seeds, for 1 minute, stirring constantly.

3. Add the mince and fry until all the liquid evaporates (about 10 minutes), stirring frequently.

4. Add the turmeric, stir and fry for 30 seconds.

5. Add the salt, cashews and the water, bring to the boil, cover the pan and cook over low heat for 15 minutes, stirring occasionally.

6. Meanwhile, put the milk into an electric liquidiser followed by the fried onions, garlic and ginger. Blend until the ingredients are smooth and stir into the mince. Bring to the boil again, cover the pan and simmer for 10-15 minutes or until the gravy is thick.

7. Put the mince onto a serving dish and garnish with the hard-boiled eggs and the coriander leaves.

TIME Preparation takes 25-30 minutes, cooking takes 40-45 minutes.

Sikandari Raan

SERVES 6-8

1½-2kg/3½-4lbs leg of lamb

*Put the following ingredients into an
electric food processor or liquidiser and
blend until smooth*

300ml/10fl oz thick set natural yogurt

1-inch cube of root ginger, peeled and
    coarsely chopped

4-6 cloves garlic, peeled and coarsely
    chopped

1 medium-sized onion, coarsely chopped

1 fresh green chilli

2 tbsps fresh mint or 1 tsp dried or bottled
    mint

*Add the following ingredients and blend
for a few seconds longer*

1 tbsp ground coriander

1 tsp ground cumin

1 tsp garam masala

1 tsp ground turmeric

1¼ tsps salt or to taste

*Grind the following 3 ingredients in a
coffee grinder*

2 tbsps white poppy seeds

1 tbsp sesame seeds

2 tbsps desiccated coconut

25g/1oz ghee or unsalted butter

450g/1lb medium-sized potatoes, peeled
    and halved

Liquidise to a smooth paste

125g/5fl oz thick set natural yogurt

50g/2oz raw cashews

50g/2oz seedless raisins, soaked in a little
    warm water for 30 minutes

1. Remove as much fat as possible from the meat and lay it flat on a board. Make deep incisions from top to bottom at about ¼ -inch intervals. These incisions should be as deep as possible, almost down to the bone. Turn the leg over and repeat the process.

2. Mix the yogurt-based mixture with the ground spices. Rub this marinade into each incision, and then fill the incisions with it. Rub the remaining marinade all over the surface of the leg of lamb on both sides. Place in a covered container and leave to marinate in the refrigerator for 48 hours. Turn it over about every 12 hours.

3. Preheat the oven to 230°C/450°F/Gas Mark 8. Place the leg of lamb on a roasting tin, melt the ghee or butter and pour it over the meat. Cover the meat with aluminium foil or use a covered roasting dish and cook in the centre of the oven for 20 minutes. Reduce heat to 190°C/375°F/Gas Mark 5 and cook for 30 minutes. Now add the potatoes and spoon some of the spiced liquid over them as well as over the meat. Cover and cook for a further 35-40 minutes, basting the meat and the potatoes occasionally.

4. Now pour the liquidised nut mixture over the meat, cover and return the meat to the oven for about 30 minutes, basting the meat and the potatoes as before.

5. Transfer the meat onto a serving dish and arrange the potatoes around it. Spoon any remaining liquid over the meat and the potatoes. The meat is served cut into chunky pieces rather than thin slices.

TIME Preparation takes 25-30 minutes plus time needed for marinating,
cooking takes 1 hour 45 minutes – 2 hours.

MARINATED LAMB CHOPS

This is an excellent way to cook lamb chops though a little unusual. The chops are tender and juicy and the gravy, thickened with a leaf spinach, is delicious.

SERVES 4-6

1kg/2.2lbs lamb chump chops

125g/5oz thick set natural yogurt

1-inch cube of root ginger, peeled and coarsely chopped

2-3 cloves garlic, peeled and coarsely chopped

1-2 fresh green chillies, seeded and coarsely chopped

2 tbsps cooking oil

6 green cardamoms, split open the top of each pod

Combine the following 5 ingredients in a bowl

1 tbsp ground coriander

1 tsp ground cinnamon

1 tsp ground turmeric

¼ tsp chilli powder

1 tsp paprika

175ml/6fl oz warm water

1¼ tsps salt or to taste

1. Trim off excess fat from the chops, wash and pat them dry. Flatten the chops slightly by beating them with a meat mallet. This will help tenderise and absorb the spices better.

2. Put the yogurt, ginger, garlic and green chillies in an electric liquidiser and blend until smooth.

3. Pour the yogurt marinade over the chops and mix thoroughly. Cover the container and allow the chops to marinate in a cool place for 4-6 hours or overnight in the refrigerator.

4. Heat the oil over medium heat, when the oil is hot, remove the pan from heat and add the cardamoms and the combined spices. Stir the ingredients once and place the pan back on heat.

5. Add the chops, adjust heat to high and stir and fry the chops for 4-5 minutes.

6. Add the water and salt, bring to the boil, cover the pan and simmer until the chops are nearly tender (35-40 minutes).

7. Meanwhile, prepare the spinach

2 tbsps cooking oil

1 tsp cumin seeds

2-3 cloves garlic, peeled and finely chopped

1 tsp ground cumin

1 large onion, finely sliced

450g/1lb leaf spinach; or 225g/8oz frozen (defrosted and drained) chopped

1. Heat the oil over medium heat and fry the cumin seeds until they start popping.

2. Add the garlic and ground cumin and immediately follow with the onions. Fry until the onions are lightly browned (8-10 minutes), stirring frequently.

3. Add the spinach and stir fry over medium-high heat for 1-2 minutes, then stir it into the chops.

4. Cover the pan and simmer for 20-25 minutes. Remove from heat.

Nawabi Kheema Pilau

*A rich rice dish in which mince is transformed into a wonderfully fragrant pilau
by the addition of saffron, rose water and fried nuts.*

SERVES 4-6

275g/10oz basmati rice

50g/2oz ghee or unsalted butter

1 tbsp extra ghee or unsalted butter

25g/1oz sultanas

25g/1oz raw cashews, split into halves

2 tbsps milk

1 tsp saffron strands

6 green cardamons, split open the top of
   each pod

4 whole cloves

1 tsp cumin seeds

2 bay leaves, crumpled

1-inch cube of root ginger, peeled and
   grated

2-3 cloves garlic, peeled and crushed

1-2 fresh green chillies, finely chopped and
   seeded if a milder flavour is preferred

1 tsp ground nutmeg

1 tsp ground cinnamon

1 tsp ground cumin

1 tbsp ground coriander

450g/1lb lean minced lamb

570ml/1 pint water

1½ tsps salt or to taste

150ml/5fl oz single cream

2 tbsps rosewater

2 hard-boiled eggs, sliced

1. Wash and soak basmati rice in cold water
for ½ hour, then drain.

2. Melt the 1 tbsp ghee or butter over low
heat and fry the sultanas until they swell up,
then remove with a slotted spoon and keep
aside.

3. In the same fat, fry the cashews until they
are lightly browned, remove with a slotted
spoon and keep aside.

4. Boil the milk, add the saffron strands and
put aside. Alternatively, put the milk and
the saffron strands in the microwave and
boil on full power or about 45 seconds. Set
aside.

5. Melt the remaining ghee or butter gently
over low heat and fry the cardamoms,
cloves, cumin seeds and the bay leaves for 1
minute.

6. Add the ginger, garlic and green chillies
and stir fry for 30 seconds.

7. Add all the nutmeg, ground cinnamon,
cumin and coriander and fry for 1 minute.

8. Add the mince and adjust heat to
medium. Stir and fry the mince until all
liquid dries up and it is lightly browned.
This will take about 5 minutes.

9. Add the rice, stir and fry for about 5
minutes.

10. Add the water, salt, cream and the
steeped saffron. Stir and mix well. Bring the
liquid to the boil, cover the pan and simmer
for 12-15 minutes without lifting the lid.
Remove the pan from the heat and keep it
undisturbed for a further 10-15 minutes.

11. Add half the nuts and raisins to the rice,
then sprinkle the rosewater evenly on top.
Using a fork, stir and mix in the ingredients
gently.

12. Put the pilau in a serving dish and
garnish with the remaining nuts and raisins
and the sliced hard-boiled eggs.

TIME Preparation takes 20-25 minutes, cooking takes 40-45 minutes.

Meat Maharaja

A rich lamb curry cooked in the style favoured by the great Maharajas of India. Ground poppy seeds and almonds are used to thicken the gravy and also to add a nutty flavour.

SERVES 4-6

4 tbsps ghee or unsalted butter

2 large onions, coarsely chopped

1-inch cube of root ginger, peeled and coarsely chopped

4-6 cloves garlic, peeled and coarsely chopped

1 fresh green chilli, seeded and chopped

1-2 dried red chillies, chopped

125g/5oz thick set natural yogurt

1 tsp black cumin seeds or caraway seeds

Mix the following 4 ingredients in a small bowl

3 tsps ground coriander

1 tsp garam masala

1 tsp ground turmeric

¼ tsp ground black pepper

2 tbsps white poppy seeds, ground in a coffee grinder

1kg/2.2lbs leg of lamb, cut into 1-inch cubes

1¼ tsps salt or to taste

2 tbsps ground almonds

2 tbsps chopped coriander leaves

1 tbsp lemon juice

25g/2oz unsalted pistachio nuts, lightly crushed

1. Melt 2 tbsps ghee from the specified amount over medium heat and fry the onions, ginger, garlic, green and red chillies until the onions are just soft (3-4 minutes). Remove from heat and allow to cool slightly.

2. Put the yogurt into an electric blender or food processor, add the onion mixture and blend to a purée. Keep aside.

3. Heat the remaining ghee or butter over low heat (do not overheat ghee) and add the black cumin or caraway seeds followed by the spice mixture and the ground poppy seeds. Stir and fry for 1 minute.

4. Add the meat, adjust heat to medium-high, stir and fry until meat changes colour (4-5 minutes). Cover the pan and let the meat cook in its own juice for 15 minutes. Stir occasionally during this time.

5. Add the blended ingredients and mix thoroughly. Rinse out blender container with 175ml/6fl oz warm water and add this to the meat. Stir in the salt and bring the liquid to the boil, cover the pan and simmer until the meat is tender. Stir occasionally during the first half of cooking time, but more frequently towards the end to ensure that the thickened gravy does not stick to the bottom of the pan.

6. Stir in the ground almonds and half the coriander leaves, cook, uncovered for 2-3 minutes.

7. Remove the pan from heat and add the lemon juice, mix well. Garnish with the remaining coriander leaves and sprinkle the crushed pistachio nuts on top.

KHUMBI AUR BESAN KI BHAJI

The use of mushrooms is somewhat limited in Indian cooking. However, in the West the abundant supply of mushrooms throughout the year makes it possible to create mouthwatering dishes at any time.

SERVES 4

325g/12oz white mushrooms
2 tbsps cooking oil
2-3 cloves garlic, peeled and crushed
½ tsp salt or to taste
½ tsp chilli powder
2 tbsps finely chopped coriander leaves
1 tbsp lemon juice
2 tbsps besan (gram flour or chick pea flour), sieved

1. Wash the mushrooms and chop them coarsely.

2. Heat the oil over medium heat and add the garlic. Allow garlic to turn slightly brown and add the mushrooms, stir and cook for 2 minutes.

3. Add salt, chilli powder and coriander leaves, stir and cook for 1 minute.

4. Add the lemon juice and mix well.

5. Sprinkle the besan over the mushroom mixture, stir and mix immediately. Remove from heat.

TIME Preparation takes 15 minutes, cooking takes 6-8 minutes.

SERVING IDEAS Serve as a side dish.
Suitable for freezing.

SAAG BHAJI

Spinach simmered in spices and combined with diced, fried potatoes.

SERVES 4-6

6 tbsps cooking oil

½ tsp black mustard seeds

1 tsp cumin seeds

8-10 fenugreek seeds (optional)

1 tbsp curry leaves

2-3 cloves garlic, peeled and finely chopped

2-4 dried red chillies, coarsely chopped

450g/1lb fresh leaf spinach or 225g/8oz frozen leaf spinach finely chopped

1 tbsp ghee or unsalted butter

1 large potato, peeled and diced

1 large onion, finely sliced

½ tsp ground turmeric

1 tsp ground cumin

½ tsp garam masala

¼-½ tsp chilli powder

2-3 ripe tomatoes, skinned and chopped

1 tsp salt or to taste

1. Heat 2 tbsps oil from the specified amount over medium heat and fry mustard seeds until they pop.

2. Add the cumin seeds, fenugreek (if used) and curry leaves and immediately follow with the garlic and red chillies. Allow garlic to turn slighly brown.

3. Add the spinach, stir and mix thoroughly. Cover and simmer for 15 minutes stirring occasionally.

4. Melt the ghee or butter over medium heat and brown the diced potatoes. Remove from heat and keep aside.

5. Heat the remaining oil over medium heat and fry onions until well browned (about 10 minutes), take care not to burn the onions or they will taste bitter.

6. Adjust heat to minimum and add turmeric, cumin, garam masala and chilli powder, stir and fry for 2-3 minutes.

7. Add the spinach, potatoes, tomatoes and salt, cover and simmer for 10 minutes or until the potatoes are tender, stirring occasionally. Remove from heat.

TIME Preparation takes 25-30 minutes, cooking takes 50 minutes.

AUBERGINE RAITA

For this recipe, the aubergine is traditionally cooked over charcoal or burnt-down ashes of a wood fire. If you are having a barbecue, then by all means, cook the aubergine on the coals. For the recipe below, grilled aubergine has been used.

SERVES 6-8

1 aubergine (325g/12oz)

½ tsp salt or to taste

½-inch cube of root ginger, peeled and coarsely chopped

1 fresh green chilli, coarsely chopped and seeded for a milder flavour

125g/5oz thick set natural yogurt

2-3 tbsps finely chopped onions

2 tbsps chopped coriander leaves

1. Make one or two small incisions in the aubergine to prevent it from bursting during cooking.

2. Preheat grill to medium. Grill whole aubergine for 10 minutes, turning it over once. Allow to cool completely.

3. Add the salt to the ginger and green chilli and crush them to a pulp.

4. Slit the aubergine lengthwise into two halves and scoop out the flesh. Chop the flesh finely or mash it.

5. Beat the yogurt until smooth. Add ginger/chilli/salt mixture. Stir and mix well. Add the aubergine and mix thoroughly.

6. Stir in the onions and half the coriander leaves just before serving. Garnish with the remaining coriander leaves.

TIME Preparation takes 10 minutes, cooking takes 10 minutes.

WATCHPOINT It is important to preheat the grill and cook the aubergine for the specified time. If the aubergine is not well cooked, it will be difficult to scoop out the flesh.

CABBAGE WITH CINNAMON

Cinnamon fried with onions has a rather distinctive and delicious flavour. The dish is not particularly spicy, but this combination gives it a special touch.

SERVES 4-6

4 tbsps cooking oil

1 large onion, finely sliced

2 fresh green chillies, sliced lengthwise; seeds removed if a milder flavour is preferred

3 cinnamon sticks, each 2-inches long; broken up into 2-3 pieces

1 large potato, peeled and cut into 1-inch cubes

½ tsp ground turmeric

¼ tsp chilli powder

125ml/4fl oz warm water

1 small white cabbage, finely shredded

1 tsp salt or to taste

1 tbsp chopped coriander leaves

1. Heat the oil over medium heat and fry the onions, green chillies and cinnamon sticks until the onions are soft (about 5 minutes).

2. Add the potatoes, stir and fry on low heat for 6-8 minutes.

3. Stir in the turmeric and chilli powder.

4. Add the water and bring it to the boil, cover the pan and simmer until the potatoes are half cooked (6-8 minutes).

5. Add the cabbage and salt, stir and mix well. Lower the heat to minimum setting, cover the pan and cook until the vegetables are tender (the cabbage should not be mushy). The finished dish should be fairly moist but not runny. If there is too much liquid left in the pan, take the lid off and let the liquid evaporate.

6. Stir in the coriander leaves and remove the pan from heat.

TIME Preparation takes 25 minutes, cooking takes 25 minutes.

TO FREEZE If you wish to freeze it, cook the cabbage only and add pre-boiled diced potatoes during reheating.

VARIATION For a colourful look, add 50g/2oz frozen garden peas.

GOBI ALOO

Gobi Aloo, or cauliflower with potatoes, is a classic north Indian dish. The potatoes are first boiled and the cauliflower is blanched. The two are then braised together gently with a few spices to give it a subtle but distinctive flavour.

SERVES 4-6

3 medium-sized potatoes
1 medium-sized cauliflower
5 tbsps cooking oil
½ tsp black mustard seeds
½ tsp cumin seeds
12-15 fenugreek seeds
1-2 dried red chillies, coarsely chopped
1 medium-sized onion, coarsely chopped
1 fresh green chilli, coarsely chopped
½ tsp ground turmeric
½ tsp ground cumin
1 tsp ground coriander
1¼ tsp salt or to taste
1 tbsp chopped coriander leaves (optional)

1. Boil the potatoes in their jacket and allow to cool thoroughly. The potatoes can be boiled and left in the refrigerator for 2-3 days.

2. Peel the potatoes and cut them into 2-inch squares.

3. Blanch the cauliflower in boiling water for 2 minutes, do not over-boil the cauliflower as it should remain firm after cooking. Allow the cauliflower to cool and cut it into ½-inch diameter florets.

4. Heat the oil over medium heat in a wide shallow pan, preferably non-stick or cast iron.

5. Add the mustard seeds, and as soon as they begin to pop, add the cumin and fenugreek seeds and then the red chillies.

6. Add the onions and the green chilli, stir and fry until the onions are golden brown (8-10 minutes).

7. Add the cauliflower, reduce heat to low, cover the pan and cook for 6-8 minutes.

8. Add the potatoes, turmeric, cumin, coriander and salt. Stir gently until all the ingredients are mixed thoroughly. Cover the pan and cook until the potatoes are heated through (6-8 minutes).

9. Stir in the coriander leaves (if used) and remove from the heat.

TIME Preparation takes 25-30 minutes, cooking takes 15-20 minutes.

SERVING IDEAS Serve as an accompaniment to any meat or chicken curry.

TO FREEZE Freeze before adding the potatoes. Add the potatoes during reheating.

VARIATION Add 100g/4oz frozen garden peas with the cauliflower.

POTATOES WITH POPPY SEEDS

*This quick and easy, but thoroughly delicious, potato dish comes from Assam.
Serve it as a side dish or as a snack – simply gorgeous!*

SERVES 4-6

5 tbsps cooking oil
½ tsp Kalonji (onion seeds), optional
1 tsp cumin seeds
4-6 cloves garlic, peeled and crushed
1 tsp freshly ground black pepper
½ tsp ground turmeric
700g/1½lbs potatoes, peeled and diced
1 fresh green chilli, finely chopped
6 tbsps white poppy seeds
1 tsp salt or to taste

1. Heat the oil in a non-stick or cast iron pan until smoking. Remove the pan from heat and add the kalonji (if used) and cumin seeds.

2. As soon as the seeds start crackling, add the garlic and place the pan over medium heat.

3. Add the ground black pepper and turmeric, stir briskly and add the potatoes and the green chilli. Fry the potatoes for 2-3 minutes stirring constantly.

4. Reduce heat to low, cover the pan and cook until the potatoes are tender (12-15 minutes), stirring occasionally.

5. Meanwhile, grind the poppy seeds in a coffee grinder into a coarse mixture. Add this to the potatoes, adjust heat to medium and fry the potato and poppy seed mixture for 5-6 minutes, stirring frequently.

6. Stir in the salt and remove the pan from heat.

TIME Preparation takes 10 minutes, cooking takes 20 minutes.

WATCHPOINT Make sure the potatoes are cut into small cubes, if cut into chunky pieces it will be difficult to cook them thoroughly in the specified time.
Use a non-stick or cast iron pan, otherwise the potatoes will stick.

CUCUMBER RAITA

*This raita is rather cooling and the aroma of the roasted cumin seeds
is very appetizing.*

SERVES 4-6

1 small cucumber
1 tsp cumin seeds
125g/5oz thick set natural yogurt
¼ tsp salt
¼ tsp paprika

1. Peel the cucumber and cut lengthwise into two halves. Slice each half finely.

2. Heat a small pan over low heat and dry roast the cumin seeds until they turn a shade darker. Allow the seeds to cool, then crush them with a rolling pin or pestle and mortar.

3. Beat the yogurt until smooth. Stir in the cumin along with the salt.

4. Reserve a few slices of cucumber for garnish and add the rest to the yogurt – mix thoroughly.

5. Put the raita into a serving dish and arrange the reserved cucumber on top.

6. Sprinkle the paprika evenly on the sliced cucumber.

TIME Preparation takes 15 minutes.

VARIATION Add half cucumber and half finely sliced radish.

Onion Relish

Raw onions with chillies and lemon juice, often accompany an Indian meal. The flavour of raw onions can be rather strong; if you prefer a milder flavour, wash the chopped onions in cold water and drain them first.

SERVES 4-6

225g/8oz onions, finely chopped
1 fresh green chilli, seeded and minced
1 tbsp fresh mint, minced
1 tbsp fresh coriander leaves, minced
½ tsp salt or to taste
1 tbsp lemon juice

1. Mix all the ingredients together except salt.

2. Stir in the salt just before serving.

TIME Preparation takes 10-15 minutes.

SERVING IDEAS Serve with all types of Kababs, Biriani or Tandoori Chicken, and with rice and meat or chicken curry.

TOMATO & CUCUMBER SALAD

*This salad, with its combination of cucumber, tomato and roasted peanuts
makes a mouthwatering side dish.*

SERVES 4-6

½ a cucumber

2 tomatoes

1 bunch spring onions, coarsely chopped

1 tbsp lemon juice

1 tbsp olive oil

¼ tsp salt

¼ tsp freshly ground black pepper

1 tbsp chopped coriander leaves

25g/1oz roasted salted peanuts, crushed

1. Peel the cucumber and chop finely.

2. Chop the tomatoes finely.

3. Put cucumber, tomatoes and spring onions into a serving bowl.

4. Combine the lemon juice, olive oil, salt, pepper and coriander leaves and keep aside.

5. Just before serving, stir in the peanuts and the dressing.

TIME Preparation takes 10 minutes.

SERVING IDEAS Serve with any meat, fish, chicken or vegetable curry.

VARIATION Omit the lemon juice and use 3 tbsps natural yogurt.

SAAGWALLA DHAL

Spinach and skinless split moong dhal complement each other extremely well.
The dish is easy to make and full of essential nutrients. Moong dhal is sold by
Indian grocers, but if you cannot get it, use yellow split peas.

SERVES 6-8

170g/6oz skinless split moong dhal or
    yellow split peas
2 heaped tbsps ghee or unsalted butter
1 large onion, finely sliced
1 fresh green chilli, sliced lengthwise,
    seeded for a milder flavour
2 cinnamon sticks, 2-inch long each; broken
    up into 2-3 pieces
½ tsp ground turmeric
½ tsp garam masala
¼ tsp chilli powder
1 tsp salt or to taste
1 tsp ground cumin
2 ripe tomatoes, skinned and chopped
570ml/20fl oz warm water
2 tbsps cooking oil
½ tsp black mustard seeds
2-3 cloves garlic, peeled and finely
    chopped
1-2 dried red chillies, coarsely chopped
100g/4oz frozen leaf spinach, defrosted and
    finely chopped or 275g/10oz fresh
    spinach; hard stalks removed and finely
    chopped

1. Wash and soak the dhal for 1½-2 hours and drain well.

2. Melt the ghee or butter over medium heat in a non-stick or cast iron pan and fry the onions, green chilli and cinnamon until the onions are lightly browned (6-8 minutes).

3. Add the turmeric and garam masala, stir and mix well.

4. Add the dhal, chilli powder and salt, stir and fry for 8-10 minutes over low heat.

5. Add the cumin and tomato, stir and cook for 3-4 minutes.

6. Add the water, bring to the boil, cover and simmer for 30-35 minutes, stirring occasionally.

7. Meanwhile, heat the oil over medium heat and fry the mustard seeds until they pop.

8. Add the garlic and allow it to turn slightly brown.

9. Add the dried red chillies and then the spinach, stir and mix thoroughly. Cover the pan and simmer for 5 minutes.

10. Add the spinach to the dhal, cover and cook over low heat for 10 minutes, stirring occasionally. Remove the pan from heat.

TIME Preparation takes 10-15 minutes plus time needed to soak the dhal,
cooking takes 1 hour 10 minutes.

BHINDI (OKRA) WITH COCONUT

A quick and delicious way to cook okra. Roasted and ground poppy and sesame seeds with coconut coat the okra and add a very special flavour.

SERVES 4

225g/8oz bhindi (okra)
2 tbsps sesame seeds
1 tbsp white poppy seeds
1-2 dried red chillies
2 tbsps desiccated coconut
1 fresh green chilli, coarsely chopped
3 tbsps cooking oil
½ tsp black mustard seeds
¼ tsp fenugreek seeds
2 cloves garlic, peeled and finely chopped
    or crushed
½ tsp salt or to taste

---

1. Wash the bhindi, trim off head and cut each bhindi into two pieces.

2. Heat an iron griddle or other heavy-based pan over medium heat and dry-roast the sesame and poppy seeds until they are lightly browned. Transfer the seeds to a plate and allow them to cool.

3. Reheat the griddle and dry-roast the coconut until the coconut is lightly browned, stirring constantly. Transfer the coconut to a plate and allow it to cool.

4. Put the sesame and poppy seeds and the dried red chillies in a coffee grinder and switch on; when half done, add the coconut and the green chilli and grind until smooth.

5. Heat the oil over medium heat and add the mustard seeds, as soon as the seeds pop add the fenugreek followed by the garlic. Allow garlic to turn slightly brown and add the bhindi and salt; stir and mix thoroughly. Lower heat to the minimum setting, cover the pan and cook for about 10 minutes, stirring occasionally.

6. Stir in the ground ingredients and mix well. Remove from the heat.

TIME Preparation takes 15-20 minutes, cooking takes 12-15 minutes.

SPICED GREEN BEANS

Sliced green beans are braised with a few spices, then tossed in roasted, ground sesame seeds to create the unique flavour of this dish.

SERVES 4-6

2 tbsps sesame seeds

3 tbsps cooking oil

¼ tsp black mustard seeds

4-6 cloves garlic, peeled and finely chopped

1-2 dried red chillies, coarsely chopped

½ tsp ground turmeric

1 tsp ground coriander

450g/1lb frozen sliced green beans, defrosted and drained

¾ tsp salt or to taste

1 tbsp desiccated coconut

1. Heat an iron griddle or other heavy-based pan over medium heat and dry-roast the sesame seeds until they are lightly browned, stirring constantly. Transfer them to a plate and allow to cool.

2. Heat the oil over medium heat and add the mustard seeds. When they begin to pop, add the garlic and allow it to turn slightly brown.

3. Add the red chillies, turmeric and coriander, stir briskly and add the beans and salt. Mix thoroughly, lower heat to minimum setting, cover the pan tightly and cook until the beans are tender (15-20 minutes), stirring occasionally.

4. Grind the sesame seeds and the coconut in a coffee grinder and stir into the beans. Remove the pan from the heat.

TIME Preparation takes 10-15 minutes, cooking takes 25-30 minutes

JEERA PANI

Jeera Pani (cumin water) has been a popular appetizer from time immemorial.
Cumin is noted for its digestive properties.

SERVES 4

2 tbsps cumin seeds
570ml/20fl oz water
2-3 dried red chillies
15g/½oz mint leaves, chopped or
    1 tsp dried mint
1 tsp salt
1 tsp sugar
1 tbsp lemon juice

1. Heat a cast iron or other heavy-based pan and dry-roast the cumin seeds until they are a shade darker, and crush them lightly.

2. Put the water in a saucepan and bring it to the boil.

3. Add the cumin, chillies, mint, salt and sugar.

4. Cover the pan and simmer for 15 minutes.

5. Stir in the lemon juice and remove from heat. Allow the drink to cool, then strain into individual glasses.

TIME Preparation takes a few minutes plus cooling the seeds, cooking takes 15 minutes.

SERVING IDEAS Serve as an appetiser or during meals. Can be served at room temperature or chilled.

MANGO SHERBET

Mango Sherbet is a delicious and nourishing drink. The quantities used here make a thick sherbet which can be thinned down by adding more milk or water as desired.

MAKES 2 pints

1 × 450g/1lb can of mango pulp
or 2 × 425g/15oz cans of sliced mangoes,
    drained
570ml/20fl oz milk
4 tbsps caster sugar
1 tsp ground cardamom
1 tbsp rosewater (optional)
300ml/10fl oz cold water

1. Put the mango pulp or slices, half the milk, sugar, cardamom and rosewater into an electric liquidiser or food processor and switch on for a few seconds.

2. Transfer the contents into a large jug or bowl and add the remaining milk and the water.

3. Chill for 2-3 hours.

TIME Preparation takes a few minutes.

SERVING IDEAS Serve during meals or at a barbecue.

VARIATION Omit the milk and use all water. Top the drink with a scoop of vanilla ice cream.

SEMOLINA AND ALMOND HALVA

A quick and easy to prepare dessert which is also delicious and filling.

SERVES 6-8

100g/4oz ghee or unsalted butter
100g/4oz fine semolina
100g/4oz ground almonds
100g/4oz sugar
½ tsp ground nutmeg
300ml/10fl oz full cream milk
25g/1oz raw cashews, chopped

1. Grease a large plate and keep aside.

2. Melt the ghee or butter over low heat in a heavy-based pan.

3. Add the semolina and cook until golden brown (6-7 minutes) stirring continuously.

4. Add the almonds, sugar and the nutmeg, stir and mix thoroughly.

5. Add the milk and mix, stirring until the mixture thickens and stops sticking to the bottom and sides of the pan.

6. Put the mixture onto the greased plate and spread it evenly to about ½-inch thickness; use the back of a lightly greased metal spoon to do this. Using a knife, press the sides inwards to form a large square.

7. Sprinkle the chopped cashews evenly on top and press them in gently with the palm of your hand.

8. Allow the mixture to cool and cut into 1-inch squares.

TIME Preparation takes 5 minutes, cooking takes 15 minutes.

SERVING IDEAS Serve as a dessert or as a tea time snack.

VARIATION Omit the ground almonds and use 225g/8oz semolina.

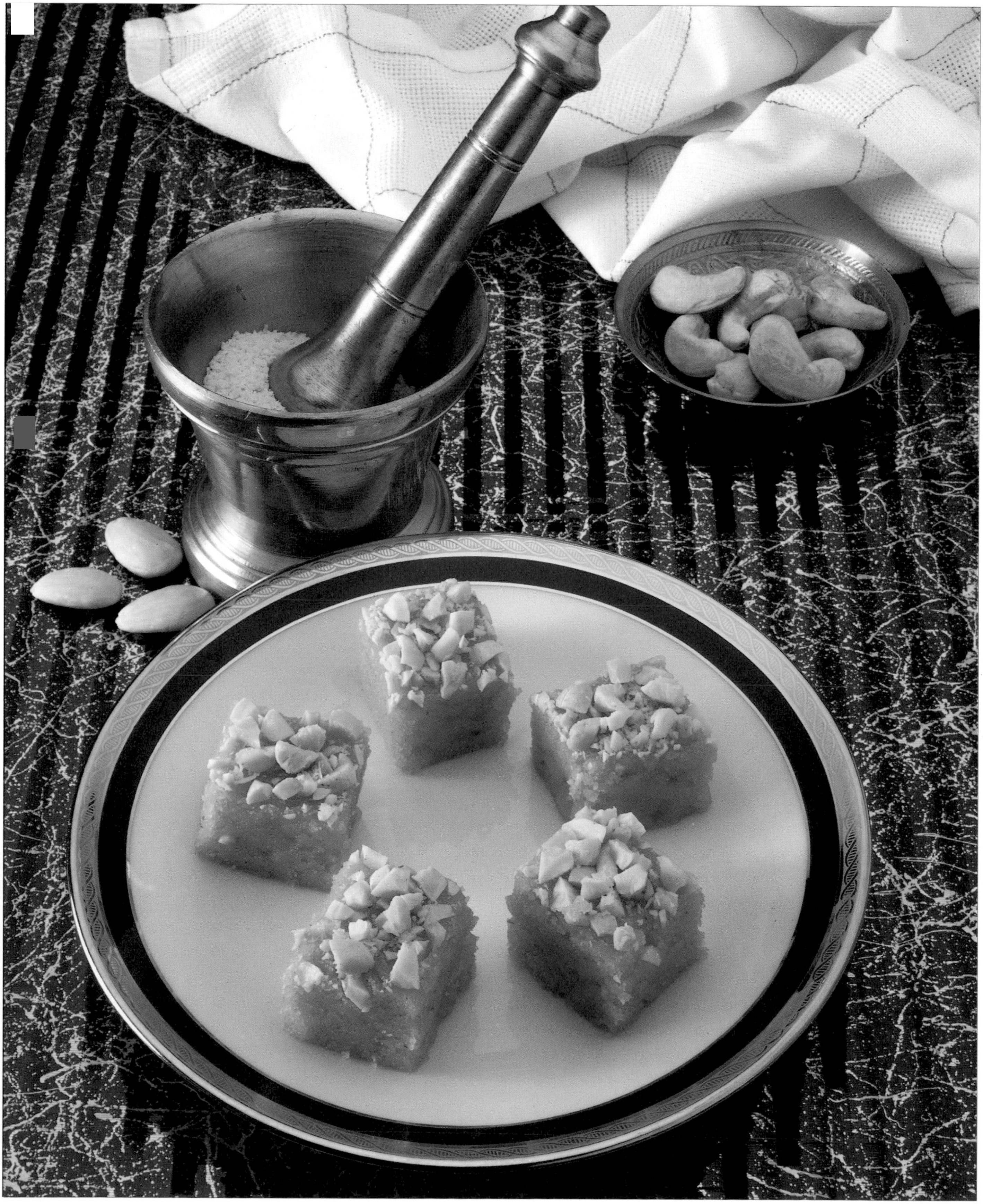

FIRNI (CREAMED GROUND RICE WITH DRIED FRUIT AND NUTS)

Although firni is basically a rice pudding, it is a far cry from the western creamed rice or rice pudding. Firni is rich, delicious and temptingly aromatic.

SERVES 6-8

300ml/10fl oz fresh milk
45g/1½oz ground rice
1 tbsp ground almonds
500g/14oz tin of evaporated milk
50g/2oz sugar
1 tbsp rosewater
1 tsp ground cardamom
25g/1oz flaked almonds
25g/1oz pistachio nuts, lightly crushed
25g/1oz dried apricot, finely chopped

1. Put the fresh milk into a heavy-based saucepan over a medium heat.

2. Mix the ground rice and ground almonds together and sprinkle evenly over the milk.

Bring the milk to the boil, stirring frequently.

3. Add the evaporated milk and sugar, stir and cook over a low heat for 6-8 minutes.

4. Remove from heat and allow the mixture to cool – stirring occasionally to prevent skin from forming on top.

5. Stir in the rosewater and the ground cardamom.

6. Reserve a few almonds, pistachios and apricots and stir the remainder into the pudding.

7. Transfer the firni into a serving dish and top with the reserved fruit and nuts. Serve hot or cold.

TIME Preparation takes 5-10 minutes, cooking takes about 15 minutes.

VARIATION Add a few raw cashews (coarsely chopped) while cooking the ground rice and ground almonds.

SHRIKAND

Shrikand is a delicious and creamy dessert which is made of strained yogurt. The yogurt is tied and hung until all the water content has drained off, the result being a thick and creamy yogurt which is rich but delicious.

SERVES 6

3 × 425g/15oz cartons of thick set natural
   yogurt
¼ tsp saffron strands
1 tbsp hot water
75g/3oz caster sugar
1 heaped tbsp ground almonds
½ tsp ground cardamom
¼ tsp grated or ground nutmeg

1. Pour the yogurt onto a clean, very fine muslin cloth; bring together the four corners of the cloth so that the yogurt is held in the middle. Tie the four corners into a tight knot and hang the muslin over the sink until all the water content has been drained off; 4-6 hours or undisturbed overnight.

2. Add the saffron strands to the hot water, cover and keep aside.

3. Untie the muslin cloth carefully and empty the contents into a mixing bowl. Beat the strained yogurt with a fork, or a wire beater, until smooth.

4. Add the sugar, beat and mix thoroughly. Add the ground almonds, cardamom and the nutmeg and mix well.

5. Stir in the saffron strands and the water in which it was soaked.

6. Chill before serving.

TIME Preparation takes a few minutes plus time needed to drain the yogurt.

VARIATION Top the Shrikand with mandarin orange segments, sliced mangoes or chopped pistachio nuts.

STUFFED LYCHEES

Lychees grow abundantly in India and the fruit is normally eaten on its own, when ripe. In this recipe you can use tinned fruit to produce this delicious and refreshing dish.

SERVES 4-6

2 × 425g/15oz cans lychees, sweetened

1 fresh mango or 425g/15oz canned sliced mangoes

2 tbsps cornflour

2 tbsps lemon juice

The finely grated rind of 1 lemon

150ml/5fl oz double cream

1 heaped tbsp ground almonds

A few drops of yellow food colouring (optional)

Roasted flaked almonds to decorate (optional)

1. Drain the lychees and the mangoes and reserve 175ml/6fl oz lychee and 125ml/4floz mango syrup. Mix the syrups together and keep aside. If using fresh mango, reserve all the juice from the lychees and make up to 300ml/10fl oz by adding cold water.

2. Put the cornflour into a saucepan and add a little syrup to make a smooth paste. Gradually add the rest of the syrup and mix thoroughly.

3. Add the lemon rind and juice and cook over low heat until the mixture thickens. Allow to cool.

4. Beat the cream until thick, and stir into the cornflour mixture along with the food colouring. Add the ground almonds and mix well.

5. Remove any broken lychees, chop them finely and mix with the cornflour mixture. Reserve whole lychees.

6. Chop the mango slices coarsely.

7. Stuff each whole lychee with chopped mangoes in such a way that the mango stands about ¼-inch high on each lychee.

8. Mix any remaining mango pieces or pulp with the cornflour mixture.

9. Line a 10-inch flan dish with the cornflour mixture and arrange the lychees on top (the cornflour mixture will line a smaller dish rather thickly and therefore cause the lychees to sink).

10. Chill before serving.

TIME Preparation takes 20-25 minutes.

SERVING IDEAS As it is light and refreshing, it will round off any Indian meal extremely well.

VARIATION Use fresh strawberries instead of mangoes.

DURBARI MALPURA

A great delicacy from the courts of the Mughal Emperors, these small pancakes are smothered with dried fruits and nuts and cream, and delicately flavoured with nutmeg and orange rind.

SERVES 6

75g/3oz plain flour
25g/1oz ground rice
50g/2oz caster sugar
1 tsp ground or finely grated nutmeg
Pinch of bicarbonate of soda
Finely grated rind of 1 orange
25g/1oz each of raw cashews and walnuts, lightly crushed
125ml/4fl oz full cream milk
Oil for deep frying
1 tsp butter
25g/1oz sultanas
25g/1oz flaked almonds
300ml/10fl oz single cream
1 tbsp rose water

1. Put the flour, ground rice, sugar, nutmeg, soda bicarbonate, orange rind and the crushed nuts into bowl.

2. Add the milk and stir until a thick batter is formed.

3. Heat the oil over medium heat in a deep frying pan.

4. Put in 1 heaped teaspoon of the batter at a time until the whole pan is filled with a single layer.

5. When the malpuras (spoonfuls of batter) start floating to the surface, turn them over. Fry gently until golden brown on both sides (about 5 minutes). Drain on absorbent paper.

6. Melt the butter over low heat and fry the sultanas for 1 minute. Remove them with a slotted spoon and drain on absorbent paper.

7. In the same fat, fry the almonds until they are lightly browned. Drain on absorbent paper.

8. Put the cream in a saucepan, large enough to hold all the malpuras and bring to a slow simmer.

9. Put in the malpuras and stir gently.

10. Turn the entire contents of the pan onto a serving dish and sprinkle the rosewater evenly on top.

11. Garnish with the fried sultanas and the almonds. Serve hot or cold.

TIME Preparation takes 10 minutes, cooking takes 20 minutes.

VARIATION Use lemon rind instead of orange.

Index